My World Your World

Everybody Needs Water

by Ellen Lawrence

Ruby Tuesday Books

Published in 2015 by Ruby Tuesday Books Ltd.

Copyright © 2015 Ruby Tuesday Books Ltd.

Editor: Mark J. Sachner
Designer: Emma Randall
Production: John Lingham

Photo credits:
Alamy: 7, 10–11, 12, 14–15, 22; Arctic Photo: 9, 22; Corbis: 5 (bottom), 13, 22; FLPA: 6, 22; FogQuest: 20 (bottom), 21, 22; Shutterstock: Cover (Marie Havens), 2 (Marie Havens), 4, 5 (top left), 5 (top right: vinhdav), 8, 16–17 (Gilles Paire), 18 (africa924), 19 (Pal Teravagimov), 20 (top), 22, 23 (Pal Teravagimov).

Library of Congress Control Number: 2014958143

ISBN 978-1-910549-08-7

Printed and published in the United States of America

For further information including rights and permissions requests, please contact our Customer Service Department at 877-337-8577.

The picture on the front cover of this book shows boys enjoying bathing in small bowls of water. The boys live in Uganda, in Africa.

Contents

Words shown in **bold** in the text are explained in the glossary.

All the places in this book are shown on the map on page 22.

Water in Our World

We need water to drink.

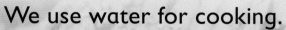

We use water for cooking.

We wash our clothes with water.

We need water to keep clean.

We use water for keeping cool and having fun.

Water in a Desert

Humans cannot survive without having water to drink.

Many people live in places where water is hard to find, however.

The San people live in the Kalahari Desert in Africa.

The San know many ways to find water in this hot, dry land.

One way is to drink rainwater that collects in small holes in trees.

This boy is using a straw made from a plant stem to drink rainwater.

The San get water from the **roots** of plants that are known as milk plants. First, they dig up a root. Then they mush up the flesh of the root and squeeze water from it.

Flesh for squeezing

Milk plant root

Water in a Frozen Land

The Nenets people live in Siberia in Russia. The temperature where they live is often much colder than inside a freezer.

The water in lakes and rivers freezes into solid ice.

Nenets people are reindeer **herders**. They live in small camps and move from place to place with their animals.

To get water, Nenets people collect snow.

Then they melt the snow over fires and stoves to make water for drinking and cooking.

A Nenets family collecting snow

Doing the Laundry

Not everyone can clean their dirty clothes in a washing machine. Many people around the world do their laundry in rivers and streams.

These women and girls in Ecuador are washing their families' clothes in a stream.

To remove water from wet clothes, people hit them hard against rocks.

The freshly washed clothes are hung outdoors to dry in the sun.

Around the world, including North America, many people hang their laundry outdoors to dry. Putting clothes in a dryer uses electricity. Drying clothes using sunshine and wind uses no electricity, so hanging laundry to dry is better for our planet.

No Clean Water

Millions of people around the world have no clean water. Many get their water from small, puddle-like waterholes, dirty streams, or **polluted** rivers. The water may contain insects and germs.

Drinking dirty water can give people **diarrhea** and other illnesses.

Every day, about 4,000 children die because dirty water has made them sick.

This young child has only dirty, muddy water to drink.

In India, millions of people in cities have no water in their homes. Each day, people must wait for hours for trucks to bring them water. Often, the trucks bring only enough water for drinking and cooking and nothing to spare for washing. Sometimes the water is dirty and makes people sick.

People bring cans and buckets to the water truck to be filled.

Walking for Water

As the Sun rises each morning, many children around the world begin their chores. Their first job is to make a long walk to collect water for their families.

Some children have to walk for an hour or more to reach a waterhole, pond, or stream.

Then they walk an hour back to home carrying a heavy can of water.

Many children have to make this journey three or four times each day!

Filling a large can with a jug or ladle takes a long time.

In many families, it is the girls' job to collect water. The girls are busy all day collecting water and doing other chores, such as cooking. They have no time to go to school or play with their friends.

These girls are collecting water in Uganda, in Africa.

15

Digging a Well

In Africa, many people, especially children, spend hours each day getting water. They would not need to do this if their village had a well. It costs a lot of money to dig a well, however.

Sometimes, **charities** help poor villages raise money to build a well.

Then **engineers** visit the village and choose a spot with water underground.

They drill into the ground and put pipes down into the water.

Drilling machine

Water pipe

Pipes carry water from deep underground to a pump on the surface. When people push the handle of the pump up and down, clean, fresh water pours out!

The village chief tries out a new water pump.

Clean Water for Everyone

Once a village in Africa has a well, it can make a difference in all the villagers' lives.

Water that comes from deep underground is clean and free of germs.

When people drink this water, they don't get sick.

It's quick work to collect water from the village well.

Having plenty of water makes it easier to grow vegetables and other crops.

Having clean water and better food makes everyone healthier.

If children don't have to spend hours collecting water, they have time to go to school. Kids who are healthy don't miss school due to illness. They also have lots of energy to study and play.

Having water for hand washing and keeping clean stops germs from spreading, too.

Turning Fog into Water

Some people live in places with little running water, but lots of fog. Fog is a cloud that touches the ground. It is made up of tiny drops of water.

To collect fog, people use a fog collector made of mesh, or net.

Fog on a hillside

A fog collector

The wind blows fog through the collector.

The tiny drops of water in fog collect on the mesh.

These fog collectors supply water to a village in Guatemala.

The water from a fog collector runs into pipes and can be used for drinking, cooking, and washing.

A large fog collector can produce about 50 gallons (190 liters) of water each day. The water is clean, so it is safe and healthy to drink.

Where in the World?

United States
Page 4

Burkina Faso
Pages 12 and 16–17

United Kingdom
Page 5

Uganda
Cover and pages 14–15

Siberia, Russia
Pages 8–9

India
Pages 11 and 13

North America

Europe

Asia

Africa

Vietnam
Page 5

Guatemala
Pages 20–21

South America

Australia

Indonesia
Page 11

Malawi
Page 18

Ecuador
Page 10

Namibia
Page 4

South Africa
Pages 6–7

Swaziland
Page 19

Australia
Page 5

Glossary

charity (CHAR-uh-tee)
An organization that raises money and uses it to do good work such as helping people living in poverty.

diarrhea (dye-uh-REE-uh)
A stomach illness that makes people's stomach ache and their poop become liquid.

engineer (en-juh-NIHR)
A person who uses math, science, and technology to design and build machines.

herder (HUR-dur)
A person who spends his or her life caring for animals that are raised for food, milk, or skins. Herders move, or herd, their animals from place to place so that the animals can find food.

polluted (puh-LOOT-id)
Made dirty and often dangerous with pollution such as trash, oil, chemicals, or even animal or human waste.

roots (ROOTSS)
Underground parts of a plant that take in water from soil. Some plants have long, thin roots. Others, such as milk plants, have fat, fleshy roots. These fleshy roots not only take in water, they store it, too.

Index

A
Africa 6–7, 14–15, 16–17, 18, 22

C
charities 16
collecting water 14–15, 16, 18–19
cooking 4, 9, 13, 15, 21

D
deserts 6–7
diarrhea 12
dirty water 12–13

drinking 4, 6–7, 9, 12–13, 18, 21

E
engineers 16

F
fog 20–21

G
germs (in water) 12, 18–19

I
ice 8
India 13, 22

K
Kalahari Desert 6–7

L
laundry 5, 10–11

N
Nenets people 8–9

P
pumps 17

S
San people 6–7
school 15, 19
Siberia, Russia 8–9, 22
snow 9

W
washing and keeping clean 5, 13, 19, 21
wells 16–17, 18

Read More

Stewart, Melissa. *Water (National Geographic Readers).* Washington, DC: National Geographic (2014).

Strauss, Rochelle. *One Well: The Story of Water on Earth (CitizenKid).* Toronto: Kids Can Press (2007).

Learn More Online

To learn more about water in our everyday lives, go to
www.rubytuesdaybooks.com/water